WILLOW

Poems of Devotion

Elizabeth Anne Hin

Copyright © 2016 Elizabeth Anne Hin

All Rights Reserved

Art Copyright © 2016 by Cynthia L. Kirkwood

Editing and Design by Sarla V. J. Matsumura

Library of Congress Control Number: 2016907045

ISBN-13: 9780692582787
ISBN-10: 0692582789

Printed in the United States of America

Published by Issa Press
Austin, Texas

DEDICATION

To Blaine Richard Glass

CONTENTS

Yogi	1
Camille	3
Grandmother	5
Hero	9
Gil	11
Brother	29
Son	33
Piaf	35
Saint Elizabeth	37
A Birthday Candle	39
Three Men	49
African Easter	55
Kabir	59
White Dove	63
Birch, Willow	67

YOGI

He
My yogi
Lit the incense
And
Bowing his head
Before
The Lord
He intoned
Any
One
Of the prayers
Of his vast and complete heart

All the day long
My yogi
Served Him
Everywhere
Served
The One
Who
Almost never
Spoke to him
Entered his dreams
Gave him
Visions
Perfumes

Or the graces
Of direct
Intact
Experience

And then
On his
My yogi's
Fifty~third
Birthday

God said
To him
I am in everything that you do
Every breath of who you are
You
Who serve Me
Everywhere
In Eternity
As do I
Who Am
All.

For Blaine Richard Glass

CAMILLE

She
walks
in grace
like a
great
gentle
saint
of
an
ancient
era

only
now.

She
has a
voice
which
even
God's
ears
tired
exhausted
from
the
suffering
of
humankind

of His
cosmos
hears
as
holy
lullabies
when
she
speaks

And
when
she
sings

I know
oh I
know
that
angels
are
here
forever
true
true
forever
loving
Camille.

For Camille Helminski

GRANDMOTHER

Grandmother,
Where did you go?

I know
your crisp mind
erudite
when you were young
scintillating
witty
kind
and
clear
thought
maybe
there
was no God
no Heaven
nothing
after this
nowhere
to go

Grandmother
where did you go?

I know
that
in my cells

your soul
cries
go ahead
and
that the pearls
of all your days
adorn
my dreams
my fears
my love
my way
forward

I
am strong
because of you
and will try
because
of you

and the ocean resounds
that it is so
and the grey blue
of the Spring
at your Cape
sky, sea, shorebird calling
is beside me
as I ask

Grandmother
where did you go?

and after the snow
the strong bite of wind
and
the dusk of winter light
as we turn to my years, my time, our time here
with your benediction
I see the tips
of a hyacinth
cupping toward Heaven,
the bloom
about to begin
just like me

the fragrance
is all about me
and I know
Grandmother
you are in Heaven
and
you are here

you are my Grandmother
my perfume
of grace
my hyacinth.

In honor of Marjorie Robbins Wallace MacLeod Pierce

HERO

There is
sometimes
in
gentleness
in
kindness
in
faithful
love
as
Spouse
and
Father
and
Son
and
Protector
to
a
Nation
at
a
time
of
war
before

and
ever
after
a
kind
of
hero.

And
he
is
one
of
ours
forever.

For Admiral Uncle Mark Tremaine

GIL

I. Boyhood

Out of the
Silence

Eight decades
And
Just over
Nine months
Ago

In the
Womb
Of a
Truly
Good woman

Surrendered
To Jesus
And God
Her God
Of Abraham
And Sarah

A seed
Was fertile

And
His Father
Moved
And the seed
Was
Made alive

In Grace
A moving
Flower
An ocean
A Word
Made
Flesh

He was
Born
And nursed
Grew
And yet

The Word
The One
The Grace
Never
Left him

There was
No veil
Of loss
And
Sorrow

We
Might say
He was
He is
God's own joy
Manifest

He
Walked
Through
Childhood
And
Youth

As
If
He were
The same
As
All children
Of his
Generation

Striped shirts
Every childhood joy
Cherished
Scolded

Blue eyes
Flaming
With eternity
Tending
The Fields
Of the Lord

For his Mother
His Father
And ancestors
For Jesus
For God
For all.

II. Youth

Whoa

I
Am
A
Man

Cigarette

Oh
That
Is
Good

I
Got
To

Go
To work

And
That
Woman
She
Is

This
Is
Love
And

Wife

And

Who
Am I

And Who
Are You
And

What
Do
I
Do
To
Put
Together
This
World

Goddammit

Give
Me
A
Cigarette

Where's
My
Shirt

I
Got
To

Go
To
Work

III. Manhood

Boy
I
Like
That
Car

Our Child
Another

Blessed
We are
Blessed

Years

Of
Wisdom
Humility
Ordinary

Life
Householder
Saint
Husband
Colleague
Father

I
Love
Her
She
Loves
Me

I am
Never
Enough
For
Her
When
Will
I
Ever
Be
Enough
For
Her
I
Was
Always

Enough
For
My
Mother

What's
Wrong
Now
What

Another
Child

Boy
I
Like
That
Car

And
I
Am
Flickering
Flame
Of the Holy Spirit
Ah
There
It is
That Bliss

No
My mind
Is just
Not
Clear
Cooperating
Go to bed
Listen to your Mother

I did

No distractions
No description
Of
Myself
Just
My

Self

I
Love
My
Wife
Look
At
Her

Isn't
She
Just
Beautiful

The
Kids
Are
Great

Boy
I
Like
That
Car

IV. Maturity

Out of the Silence
A voice is making its way
To me
I remember this voice
From before I was born
And for always

It is your voice

There was that program
Yoga
And problems with
One of my children
And that corruption
I was heartbroken
Surprised and confused and yet not
And my friend's marriage that
Just couldn't take it
He bailed

And
That seminar
Or music
Or seeking

No,
I am not seeking
I remember
Out of the Silence
A voice is making its way
To me
A voice I remember
From before I was born
And always

V. Sage

Mantra

Stillness
Temper
Grace
Silence
Duty
Marriage
World

A flower

Out of the Silence
A voice is making its way
To me
A flower
A guru
No
A flower
A garland
Mantra
Silence

VI. The Path

He is
Well he is not well

Crazy
Well
Disturbed
Or
Maybe
Emotional
Mental
Yeah
But he is
What

Is he doing
Now
Well
At least there is some money

But

And the kids are old enough
How do we hide him
Well he can work

What

And then

Stroke

Even Heaven sighs

He could accept,
You know
All the doubt
Greed,
All the reactions
To Gil
To the seeming era
At hand

And
Out of the Silence
A voice is making its way
To me
I remember this voice
From before I was born
And for always

Stillness
Mantra
Duty

Silence

VII. Dawn

Ushas, the bright eyed Goddess of the Dawn
Ma
Hail
Mary
Full of Grace

Gil
Has been born

His merit
Astounds all Buddhists

His faith
Carries the tears
Of all Christians
Beyond the cross
And the resurrection

Into the truth
And the path

And that
We all
Stand

With the Hopi
And Mount Everest, Chomolungma, Sagarmatha

Every mountain
Every vale,
Stream
Ocean
And
Star

To sing
Back
To the voice

I am here
I am
I
That
One

Dawn

For Gilbert Younger
On his 80th Birthday

BROTHER

Brother
Of
Gentleness
And grace
Is your
Name
Wind
Water
Sea
Or
Sky
You
Who
Never
Hurt
Harm
Injure
Any
One or animal
Plant
Who held
Our
Great
Uncle Michael's
Hand

When
You Were
So
Wee
Held
It fast
In
Your
Tiny hand
Of
Trust
And grace
Walking
With him
As he
Taught
You
Of tree
And
Dale
He whom Frank Lloyd Wright
Trusted
With waterfalls and cliffs
Only with Uncle Michael
Was he willing to build

Only with you coming
To Earth
Later
Younger brother
Of goodness
And grace
Was I willing
To be born.

For Peter William Hin

SON

Boy

Man

Noble

Kind

Sympathetic

Virtuous

Frightened

Uncertain

Filled with courage

To be realized

I

Love you

Son of

Sworn enemies

Make them heal.

Be my knight

And all of ours

Forever.

For John Taylor Gabriel

PIAF

Lady.
Beloved by me.
Your posture, perfection of face
The grace of your gaze
And your soul
Is a daughter to my deeper spirit
Forever.

For Kirsten Elise Gabriel

SAINT ELIZABETH

Girl
Perplexed
I love all of you
"I am so strong
Exactly
Who
Am I to be with
This great
Power
This perception
This destiny"
Forever.

For Mackenzie Meredith Gabriel

A BIRTHDAY CANDLE

I.

She descended from Heaven,
Between
Our Two World Wars
To help the Cosmos
Become
A Great Peace.

She was conceived
When my Grandparents drove a carriage,
By horse,
To market.

She was born,
Five years after women cast their first vote,
Beside that of Father,
Husband,
And son.

She was raised,
When dry winds blew the seeds from soil everywhere,
When my own Mother wore cardboard in the soles of her
    shoes,
When my Grandmother Cora owned two dresses~
One flowered, one plain.

Yet,
When my grandmother Anna dwelled in a fine home,
A ruby ring,
Lovely food, porcelain, crystal, silver, and
Lace,
On the table,
Always enough milk.

She was wed,
When love was a promise
Made forever.

She bore
Three sons,
Who bring her so much joy,
That,
It is the great secret
Of her heart.

She divorced.

There were women.
There were places between them
That
She did not want to be
At the hearts of her sons,
And after.

He simply broke the promise.

And yet,
Herb and she:
They had known love,
Deep lessons,
And three sons.

She raised
Three sons,
Well.

II.
She entered a study,
What a study . . .
Cornell University,
Ivy League,
Margaret Mead,
Barry Brazelton,
A doctorate,
A woman doctor,
Dr. Moshier.

A study
Of God,
Of education,
Of the great mystery,
Of the blessing,
Of Children.

A study of all that a child,
Any child,
Every child,
Could be.

She said,
I will become a doctor
Of that,
Of that living prayer,
Of every Child.

That is who I am,
In God.

Classes taught,
Counseling,
Mentoring;
Schools established.

She is
Esteemed,
Accomplished,
Wise,
Kind,
Sharp,
Intelligent,
Dynamic,
Perceptive,
Yankee severe,
Sparkling in wit,

Independent,
Intelligent,
Fierce,
Free
Clear,
Elusive,
Steadfast,
Loyal,
Ever questing,
Seeking love,
That is,
True love,
In all relationships,
And everywhere.

And,
Seeking God.

She is
A woman sage.

III.
An Infant boy prayed to Earth,
Prepared for,
Raised to toddlerhood,
To boyhood.
Her first grandchild,
Son of a spiritual friend,
Of a spiritual Daughter.

Grandchild of her soul and life,
Beloved,
Cherished,
Blessed.

IV.
She journeyed,
Adventured,
Friendships,
Concerts,
Monsieurs Monet and Van Gogh . . .
Dined on fare common, exotic,
With ears,
Eyes,
Palate,
Fingertips,
And feet.

Chinese silk,
Dragonflies,
Mooncakes,
Sacher Torte,
The Vienna Opera,
Taoist Temples of Kuan Yin,
The Icon of Czestochowa,
The I
Infant of Prague,
New mountain snow falling in the Alps,
T'ai Chi at dawn in Beijing parks,

    birds hanging in bamboo cages . . .
While their owners stood,
    smoking in the early morning mist.

On her own
Tender feet, unbound feet,
She stood.
She sat,
And she knelt.

In New Mexico, China, Germany, Austria, Poland,
California, New York, and Texas,
Praying for everyone,
Whether they knew
They were ready
For her living prayer,
Or not.

She always cried,
When she
Prayed
To God,
For peace.

At the base of Taos Pueblo's great mountain,
Atop China's Great Wall,
Walking within The White House,

At the ruins of Buchenwald, Bergen Belsen, Dachau, and
	Auschwitz,
Lit by a winter's full moon,
At Los Alamos and White Sands,

In churches, chapels, temples, squares, and fields,
Beside monuments,
Beneath sacred trees,
In the homes of friends,
Beside all women and men,
Beside all Elders and children,

Of history,
The present,
All future,

At Holy sites,
And sites needing to remember,
That they are Holy,
As they were
Created Holy,

With candle in hand
And grace in heart,
She wore soft blue,
Pearls,
Amber,
A silver band of children:
The ring ever upon her finger,
And Muguet des Bois,

That is,
Lilies of the Valley,
The beloved flower
Of her
And my
Childhoods.

V.
It is her birthday;
A candle is lit.
Look,
It is her heart,
Which has become,
At eight decades,
A flame of God.

For Dr. Loreen Moshier

THREE MEN

There were

Three men

You might

Say

They were

Wise

One man

In his

Youth

Yet

A man

A true

Man

As a

Man

One

Held

My heart

And

One

Man

Had

Stood

By

The path

Of my

Soul

For so

Very long
That my
Very breath
In God
Is
Safe
Beside him
Because
Of
Them
My
Three
Wise men
My daughter
Dwells
Beside me
Beside us
All
At Christmas

Every day
Now
For mankind
Is Christmas

And Peter
My brother
And Michael
In Taos
And Sedrick

My beloved
Friend
His
Skin
Like
Her
Skin
And
Like her
Soul
Flaming
All colors as one
In her
In God's
Grace
His ancestors
Brought
To America
Against
Their will
She brought
Through God's
Will
My very
Body
Rising up
From
Near death
To carry her
Home

To my wise
Men
To the
Women of
Every nation
And
Brian
Like a hawk
In the sky
Of every aspect
Of my life
And hers
Now
And
The flickers
Of faces
Before
Me
In Nairobi
In Kenya
In Africa
Praying
For me
For her
That she
Might
Come
Home
In
My arms

Believing
Hoping
Doubting
My arms
And her
I never doubting
Her
I am
Her mother
She is
My daughter
You are
My wise
Men
The wise
Men
Of her
Path
Of Christmas
Now.

For Michael Andrews
Dr. John David Gabriel
John Taylor Gabriel
Sedrick Wayne Gardner
Blaine Richard Glass
Brian Keith Hawley
Peter William Hin
And William Michael Hin

AFRICAN EASTER

It is Easter
And
You are here
Across
The
Wide
Ocean
And yet
Not
Anywhere
At all
But
Where
I
Am.
Your
Dark
Skin
Glistening
Beneath
The
African
Sun
And
Sky
And
Moon
And

My
Soul's
Skin
Luminous
Like
The
Buttercups
At
Play
The
Bluebonnets
So
Still
All
Of
Their
Color
And
Hue
Their
Variegated
Display
In
The
Fields
Of
Our
Lord
Bending

And
Swaying
For
You.
My
Daughter
Our
Daughter.
Easter.

Easter Monday

KABIR

And
when
I
did
not think
I could
go on
in Nairobi
with
the
questions
against me
alone,

I
could
perceive
your

Great
strength
at prayer,

Before
your Koran
before
God.

Your mustache
that
broad
face
handsome
clear
eyes
radiant
with
seeking

That
great
strength
at
prayer.

I
said,
I
told
you
I
would
not
fail.

How
could
I
we
fail
God?

There
is
Only
Him.

And
my
own
Beloved
asked,

Even
Sufis
have
marriage
problems?

I
answered,
not
anymore.

For Kabir Helminski

WHITE DOVE

Like a Dove
Agnes came
To me
This morning
Dead last fall, you know
In Taos
To caress me awake
She was all
White
Grey
White
Ivory
White
And dusky
And white
Like a Dove
Like the way a Dove
Is
White always
Like her painting
Like her
Points, spaces
Gestures of line and form
And all feeling, every feeling

Like her painting
Just down the stairs to the left
First one
At the left
At the LA
Art Museum and then
Some more
Further down
The walls, the halls
You had to go
You just had to go
There was something
In the museum
You were to see
In the 1980's
Driving in
From the Desert
Just for this
Something calling you
You had
Never been there
Before
This museum
And
You simply could not leave them
Cannot leave them
Never have
Apparently
Never will
Her orangepaintings

Agnes does not leave you
Ever
Her Mother did
Leave

Her soul
Dove soul
Touches me
Back to the world
Vision
Ears
Sense
Every sense
Even ineffable sense
Always ineffable sense
That part of us
Which is made of eternity
Painted
Facing
Something
Which touched me
That first
Painting
Agnes Martin
Like someone making love
To everything I am
Everything anyone is
Or ever has been
Or ever will be

From the painting
Emanating from the painting
Into everything

Teaching me
Mentoring me
Mothering me
Speaking
You know
You said
'If men were like they are now
When I was young
If I were younger now
Things might have been different'
You might have had one
A long time love
A lifetime love
And maybe a child
You have me
A Daughter
And Only God knows
How many others
You have

For Agnes Martin

BIRCH, WILLOW

At my
Counter
At my Bath
There are
Bottles
Not dear
Dear
To
My heart
And
To all
Of me

One
Stands
Next to
My favorite
My favorite
Neroli
Fleur d'Oranger
From
The deserts
Of God's world
The deserts
Which
Saved
My tender

Elegant
Strong
Humble
Holy
Life

The one
Standing
Next to
My Orange Blossom
Is Birch

There are
Northern
Birch
Of my Family
My conception
My birth
My childhood

The holy
Blueprint
Of my
Life
Ever safe
In God
The great
Birch
We planted
As a family

Died
As I entered
College
As my
Family
Of Maturity
Was taken from me
Thirty
Years
Now
Until
I
Helped God
With the
Great soul
Of the world

I found
Silver
Birch
Across
The great
Steppes
Of Russia
As I
Journeyed
By train
Through
The day

Through
The night
They shimmered
Unlike
Any trees
I had
Ever seen
Ever known
Ever loved

As I have ever
Loved
The Spirits
Of trees
They understand
You know
That which does not
Know
Anything
But the love
Of God
In Himself
And in All
And so
I know
Them
And
They know
Me

It began
With a Willow
My favorite
A Willow
At
Our cottage
At
The side
Of
The boathouse
Grown
At
An angle
Toward
The water
Which allowed
Me
A seat
High up
On her
Sweet
Sustaining trunk

I was
Always
Completely
Myself
Sitting
Upon her

She
Loved me
So fully
In complete
Consciousness
And
Understanding
Of God
So
That
I never betrayed
Her
She
My
Second
Mother
You
Might say
I knew
To be
Her
Daughter
Everywhere
And
Always

Several Men
Came
One day
To assess

The Cutting
Down
Of the
Dutch Elm
Largest in the County
Studied
By the
Arborists
At Cornell
There was
A
Disease
And almost all
Of the
Great
Eastern Elms
Left
Our Earth
Forever
I could
Feel

This
Holy death
This part
Of
My family
Resolved
In their duties
Of creation

In eternity
I sat
Perched
Like a House
Sparrow
At my
Seat
In my
Beloved
Tree
Tree of
Trees
And
Observed
In all dimensions
Of God
The Men
With
My Grandfather
William Charles'
Tree
His Beloved Elm
I was with
His
Grief
And Daddy's
Mom
Was glad
For the
Opening View

To
The Lake
The Smooth
Expanse
Of simple
Lawn
Which She
And my Father

Could now
Tend
With
Little
Raking
And
More
Sunshine
Upon
Our tiny
Cottage
Which
They Built
With
Their
Own hands
While
They carried
Me
To Earth

In my
Beloved
Mother's Womb
My Willow
Ever
At the beach
As I
Was
Safely
Delivered

Her roots
Limbs
Trunk
And Sap
My Second
Mother
My First Mother
And Father
Were
Twenty-three
When
I
Was Born
To Them
And to
My tree
All trees

The men
Spoke
With
My parents
As I sat
In
My
Second
Mother's
Limbs

The
Finger Lakes'
Breeze
Upon
My
Chatain hair
My eyes
The color
And texture
Of
Her bark

My
Shy
And strong
Skin
Senses
And soul
Ever turned

To
The Ecstasy of God
Every Breath
Of
This Life
And of

Every Breath
I have
Ever taken
In
Every
Life
And beyond
All Breath
So understood
And safe
Tenderly beloved
By
My
Second
Mother

They were
Casual
The men
And
My Beloved
Parents
At Dinner

That eve
My Parents
Said
To us
That the
Dutch Elm
Would be
Taken down
Soon
They spoke
When
And
That
The Cornell
Men
Would
Participate
My Father
And
My
Two
Brothers
Are
Cornell Men

My Mother
Worked
For The President
Of that
Ivy-bowered

University
Proudly
Happily
Before
We came
To her Womb
Her nursery
Her perfect
Home.

The Cornell men
Would take
If it were
Supported
By Our family
Several rings
From our
Great
Family tree
For studies
And archives

The tree
Would have
To be
Taken down
With
Unusual expertise

It would Require
Their best
Equipment
Men
Planning
Timing
Strength
And
Wisdom

Men
From
Up and down
The
Lake roads
Came by
And discussed
The
Great tree
As men
Of all
Generations
Like
To do

The roots
Would be
Taken
The next year
As they shriveled

And let go
Of the Tree's
Spirit

How many years
From seed
Cast by God
Before
White
Men
And women
Lived Upon
The Banks
Of that
Sacred
Seneca
Land
Two centuries
Indeed
Flowing water
And earth
Sprouting seed
To the
Very sky

We would camp
Under those
Elm
Bowers

Beneath
A Canopy
So high
It held
Perspective
For the
Very stars
And constellations
To
Our Lessons
With
My Father
Lying
Beside
Our quilts
Here are
The Pleiades
My favorite
And there, Orion
His

I insisted
To sleep
At the
Side
Of that
Broad trunk
Which stood
To
The left

Of
My
Second
Mother
Facing
The Lake

Never
Have
I known
Separation
From
Her
Or
From God
From
My Conception
To Today
Into Eternity

My parents
At dinner
Remarked
There
Is
That One
Problem

Well
They will
Just
Have
To take
Her
My Willow

My Second
Mother
Must
Be
Configured
Out of
The map

She
Rendered
Too
Much consciousness
Maneuvering
Attention
Concern
Care
So
She
Would
Be
Taken Down
First

To render
The situation
Easier
For
The
Men
Whomever
Said
It is
Supposed
To be
Easy

Can't

Well
Must

Can't
Oh, my tree
I speak
To you
In every
Language
Known
To
Any soul
Can't

Can't

Must do something
She is . . .

Can't
Isn't there
Something
There
Is Always
Something
You
Can do
~All Children
Know This~
Mom
Daddy

Well
They
Could
But
It would
Cost two
Hundred
Fifty
Dollars
1962

I will
Pay
With All

The Allowances
I Will
Ever
Earn
My
Whole
Life
I
Will
Borrow
From
One
Grandmother, and
Grandfather
And
The
Other

I
Will
Earn
When
I
Am
Grown
And pay
You
Back
Daddy
Mom

Please
You
Cannot

And
My
Tree
Was
Taken
Down

But
My
Second
Mother
Entered
My
Breath
So
That
My
Spirit
Is
The
Perfume
Of
A
Northern
Willow

Leaves
Quaking
In
The
Wind
So
Gentle
That
Tree
Of
My
Soul
You
Have
No
Idea

I rustle
Resilient
Timeless
Yet
In time
In the winds
Of God
Nurtured
By His
Sun
And Moon
Rain
Snow

And dew
My roots
Held
Passionately
By Our
Earth
My Leaves
Free
And filled
With
The songs
Of
His birds
Who make
Their nests
On
The Bowers
Of
My Heart
Sap runs
Through
My veins
Changing
Moods
And
Viscosity
With
The Seasons
Of The Year
And of Life

Last year
When
Still
I might
Have died

I found
A Himalayan
Birch
and
Gifted her
To my Brother
Peter
Whom
I cherish

Her Spirit
Called
To
Our
Holy Family
And
She sits
At the
Very
Crest
Of
His Garden

Caring
For
All
That his path
Shall
Ever be
She
Cost
Two
Hundred
Forty
Dollars
Plus
Tax
I
Believe
2004

I love
Aspen
A form
Of Birch
Which
Grow
As a Holy
Family
Indeed
Not
One
Tree

And
Another
From seed
But
Springing
From
One
Root
To
Birth
Another
From
Spirit
Through
Earth
And Elements
To
Sky
To
Adore
God and
Embody
Him
Like
Our Path
Never
Solitary
Ever
Enjoined

To
One
Another
In
His
Grace
Infinite
Eternal

No human
Who
Ever
Hurt
Me
Is
Greater
Than
The
Aspens'
Love
Because
I
Have
A
Second
Mother

She taught me
That
Although

The humans
Perceive
Me
To be
One
Soul
The Trees
Also
Birthed
Me
So
That
I Could
Find
My
Holy
Family
Those
Who
Form
A bouquet
Of God
Different
Flowers
Grasses
And Trees
One Bouquet
One
Garden

One
Forest

We have
Given
Eve's
Apple
Back
To God

Because
My
Second
Mother
Carried
Me
In Her
Destiny

She knew
Her
Daughter
Her
Holy
Child
Who
Was
To know
No
Human

Ever
Now
Separate
Who
Was
To call
This
Sacred
Destiny
Forward
Through
All trees
Of the
World
Forever

I have
Tasted
Silver
Birch
In
Inverness
Scotland
Crafted
Into
Wine
I Toast
My Second Mother

To
Her
To
All trees
To
All
My
Trees
All
God's trees
To you
All
My Holy Family

For My Family

ABOUT THE AUTHOR

Elizabeth Anne Hin studied poetry formally with George E. Dimock, Richard Wilbur, William Hoover Van Voris, Michael Benedikt, Elizabeth Hardwick, Sir Stephen Spender, and Joseph Brodsky. Her Mother read poetry aloud from *A Child's Garden of Verses* by Robert Louis Stevenson and from other cherished texts from Beth's conception through childhood. Her Father taught her through his admiration for Homer's life, work, and virtuous message, from the world's classics and histories, and from noble and heroic peoples and cultures of all nations. He practiced his faith in the equality of all men and women, and in all aspiration: 'Ad astra per aspera,' ~Seneca. Her Mother was a private living example of this virtue.

Beth has embraced poetry, from reading to writing, since youth, observing in gratitude the poetry infused in sculpture at Wellington's port in New Zealand and attending readings by Jorge Luis Borges at the 92nd Street YMCA in Manhattan, New York, Adrienne Rich in a hallowed hall of Amherst, Massachusetts, Drummond Hadley and Gary Snyder in Anchorage, Alaska, Mary Oliver at a Presbyterian Church in Dallas, Texas. She has been shown kindness in mentoring by writers from John Updike to Carlos Fuentes, Richard Erdoes to Derek Walcott; and by W. S. Merwin, who expressed to her in 1973 that he had written nearly every day since the age of 21, and requested of Beth that she do the same.

ALSO BY ELIZABETH ANNE HIN

The Grail: A Story of Issa and Yeshua, 2014
Live Oak: Poems of Texas, 2016
Jdg: Poems of Love, 2016

Published by Issa Press, Austin Texas

www.ingramcontent.com/pod-product-compliance
Lightning Source LLC
Chambersburg PA
CBHW022116090426
42743CB00008B/867